FILIBERT BAKES A PIE

Suzanne New Seely

Amazon

Copyright © 2023 Suzanne New Seely

All rights reserved

The characters and events portrayed in this book are fictitious. Any similarity to real persons, living or dead, is coincidental and not intended by the author.

No part of this book may be reproduced, or stored in a retrieval system, or transmitted in any form or by any means, electronic, mechanical, photocopying, recording, or otherwise, without express written permission of the publisher.

ISBN
ISBN

Cover design by: Paul Moore
Printed in the United States of America

For
my
husband

BIG JUICY
BLACKBERRIES

It was early morning. Filibert's stomach was growling like dogs in a trash fight! He was **hungry!**

From the kitchen window, Filibert eyed the big, fat **blackberries** growing along the mountain path.

"Yum! yum! yum!" he cried, patting his **belly**. "Those **blackberries**'ll make the yummiest pie ever!

Easy Peasie!" he cried.

"A -- **cinch!**"

With that, Filibert grabbed the big wicker basket off the shelf and, tugging his woolly reindeer hat down over his ears, he bound outside and headed toward the **blackberry** thickets.

Eyes glittering with *excitement*, Filibert got down on his knees and started to pick - *lickety split*, he would have enough **berries** to bake a pie.

His **pie** would be -

the *best*!
The **bestest** best!

in all **Dragon Land**!

Come August he would enter Dragon Land's annual pie baking contest. His blackberry pie was *sure* to win the **Blue** Ribbon!

YES!

He could see it now! There he was wearing a brand new **top** hat,

blue ribbon pinned on his chest!

Afterall, *what* could go wrong?

"**First Prize!**" Filibert cried.
"How fine!" His chest puffed out, the **brass** buttons

on his long **red** coat nearly popping off!

Faster, faster Filibert picked, his sharp claws snipping and snapping, slashing, plucking, tossing the fattest, juiciest most lucious-looking **blackberries** in the basket.

At last, the basket was full to the brim! Almost he could taste the berry's **thick**, sweet juice!

FILIBERT'S *FAIRYTALE* CASTLE PIE

Filibert decided - he would make a castle pie! It would be a sight to behold - nothing like that old run down castle perched high up on the Sprinkle Top Mountains.

No, sir!

His pie would not be ho hum - humdrum - *tha*t's for sure! It would not be a boring ole pie with a simple lattice crust!

No!

His pie would *not* be -

ordinary!

His pie would be

Spectacular!

Dazzling!

fit for a king and queen!
The crust would have a window where the **dragon queen** could look down onto to her own private pleasure **garden** filled with …

flowers …

and **lollipop** trees …

and **hedge-lined** pathways as far as the eye could see.

Filibert did not dawdle!

Bursting with

Gusta!

he popped on his tall white chef's hat, quickly knotted his apron behind his back and, with all the muster and fluster he had, he flew into a baking --

Frenzy

Of course, he knew how to make a pie! He had seen Mother Dragon make ten thousand pies - maybe more!

Anyways, even if he forgot any teensy weensy tinsy detail, he could figure it out with his good God given **dragon** brain!

A cinch!

In no time, Filibert's claws were sticky and dripping with **purple** goo. He dumped an entire bag of flour into the old yellow crockery bowl, sprinkled in a gigantic pinch and a half of salt, one walloping scoop of sugar, two ginormous dollops of butter, a jelly jar of water, and two tart lemons

- no - *three* tart lemons --

and then - *another!*

For **tang**!

For *zip*!

For *zing*!

For **good** measure!

Filibert started to mix -

and mix -

and *mix*!

He did not even a poke a claw in the filling for taste - because he *knew* for absolute sure that his pie was going to be ... going to be ...

wooonderfuul!

He could not wait!

After patting the dough into one humongous roly poly ball, he began beating and banging it hard with his fist. Then, he got out the old rolling pin Mother Dragon had given him and started smoothing the dough across the floured countertop.

"Easy enough!" Filibert cried, imagining himself a *master pastry chef*, wearing a tall puffy hat!

Next, he began shaping the dough into an *elaborate* castle. "This's even more fun than *daddle doodling* with clay," he thought. And ...

Zippety Zing!

His pie looked perfect, like puzzle pieces.

Dusted head - to- toe, tip-to-tail in flour, Filibert caught himself in the mirror.

"**Boo!**" he shouted just for spooky *fun*.

Now the dough was getting stiff and *hard* to squish and squash. But still, he mashed and twisted and rolled and shaped until his claws ached, and his tired arms dropped to his sides.

Because he did not have a *real* pie pan, Filibert lined his deep skillet with pie dough, baked it to a soft golden brown, then poured in the blackberry goo and carefully lay the beautiful castle crust across the top.

FILIBERT BAKES A PIE

The pie was *be* - *U* - *ti* - *ful*!

A fairytale castle, with crenelated walls all around to protect it from attackers!

Filibert's Castle Pie!

13

"**Excellent**!" Filibert bubbled with excitement. "How fine!" he cried, popping the castle pie in the warm oven.

In no time, Filibert's whole lair smelled delicious and warm and sweet and juicy -- and **blackberry**-eee too!

"**Yummiedy**!

Yum!

Yum!"

Filibert cried, smacking his lips hungrily. He could almost taste it!

After waiting for what seemed like forever, Filibert pulled the pie from the oven and stepped back to give it a good looking over.

His fairytale castle pie was a beautiful

golden brown. Filibert let out a **happy roar!**

Now, all his pie needed was a name. It had to be a *grand* name!
"Hmmm, hmmm, hmmm," Filibert thought pressing a claw to his lips as names bounced around in his head like colored balloons.

Elderberrry Castle **Pie**?

The Castle Pie of Sprinkle Top?

Dragon Land Castle Pie?

Buttertop Castle Pie?

As he gazed out his kitchen window, Filibert's eyes dropped to the Village of **Elderberry** below. They meandered along the path to **Sunshine** Valley -- and then, they lifted ...

Up!

Up!

UP!

to Meringue Point, Sprinkle Top Mountain's tippety tippetiest peak.

"Hmm, hmm, humm …," Filibert wondered.

But st*ill*, even after all his hard thinking, Filibert wasn't exactly sure *what* to name his pie?

"I know! he exclaimed at last - Nonsuch Castle!

Yes! Nonsuch was a fine name!

Afterall, didn't Nonsuch mean the *very* finest? And, because his pie was sure to be just that - the very - *very* finest of finest, the finest of finest fines, Nonsuch was the perfect name!

THE **PIE** PARTY

FILIBERT BAKES A PIE

Because Filibert was SO proud of his castle pie, he decided to have a pie party!

Yes, a pie party would be FUN!"

Fllibert rested his jaw in his hand. How he wished he could invite *all* of his friends, both **dragons** *and* human children too … oh, what a **lively mix** that would be!

-- but his lair was *too* small!

Grandfather Dragon couldn't come. He was away visiting relatives in faraway Calcutta. Nor, could Uncle **Blue**stocking **Dragon** come, as he was off vacationing on the Isle of Wight, swimming in the **deep blue sea**.

Aside from Mother Dragon and Filamina and Montaclur Dragon and Filibert's jolly-faced, buck-toothed Uncle Pinkie Pinkerton, he would, invite dandelion-haired Wilkie and Finny, Lizzie and Fiona, and her little sister, Pansy, and a smathering of his other human friends --

FILIBERT BAKES A PIE

Filibert was atwitter with

excitement!

19

"How fine!" he exclaimed.

8

9

10!" he counted.

"Yes! **Ten** would make a perfect pie party!"

The next afternoon, Filibert placed an enormous vase of freshly cut **flowers** in the center of the table.

"*Pretty*!" he thought. Just like a Van Gogh painting!

While waiting for his guests to arrive, and because he had ants in his pants, Filibert twirled and whirled, doing the closest thing he knew to dancing. Oh! What a **jolly** good time they were going to have!

In no time, his guests began arriving one by one dressed in their very finest, Uncle Bucky in his Sunday suit, his usual high Pompadour tucked beneath a fine feathered **fedora**.

"How fine!" Filibert exclaimed seeing Mother Dragon take her place at the dining room table wearing the pretty **pinky-lavender** frock and frothy hat he had made for her to wear to the **Dragon Fashion Show**.

Six of the guests were there!

Eyes shining with excitement, Filibert watched his guests bite into their slices of pie.

Then --
he waited and waited .... for compliments,
a little praise - ***something!***

but --

Not a *peep* was heard!

Suddenly, Finney's eyes popped out, and his lips rolled back so far he looked like he'd swallowed a **frog!**

"Water!" he croaked. "Water!

I'm going to be *sick*!"

Waving her hands wildly over her head, Lizzie hollered,

"**Help!** You're poisoning us! This pie tastes like an ant hill!!"

Eyes bulging, Finney let out a loud,

"**Mud**!**YUCKERS**!"

Montaclur Dragon's huge dragon **snout** scrunched, and he started belly laughing so hard, big dragon tears rolled down his wide **cheeks.**

Mother Dragon, in her usual dainty way, nibbled a teensy, weensy bite. Eyelashes fluttering as she tried swallowing, she gave a curious twist of her head. Her motherly eyes dropped to her lap. After a moment, she glanced up at her dear boy, Filibert, and with the sweetest, tenderest smile, she exclaimed,

"Fiddleybit, my dear Filibert, I declare this is the *best* pie I have ever eaten! Yes, it is *remarkable* - simply *remarkable!*"

(Filibert, Mother Dragon's dearly darling, could do NO wrong in her eyes)

Meanwhile, Uncle Pinkie Pinkerton's big beaver teeth kept munching and crunching - when - **suddenly** his eyes bulged and his dragon lips puckered out so far, he could not speak!

Filamina, the sensitive dragon that she was, dabbed her snout with her napkin. "*La dee da*, Filibert," she sang breezily. "Your pie's the most pleasantest mix alright - sweet and lemony too!"

Face turning bright burning hot, Filibert hung his head!

He knew that Mother Dragon and Filamina were just being *nice*!
    And then, wouldn't you know, here came that nosey ole **Troubling Wind**!

"Why cant' you just mind your own beeswax?" Filibert thought, his mouth *twist*ing angrily.

That busybody ole Troubling Wind *always has to have* **something** *to say*!

"Filibert! You can do better!" the Troubling Wind blew hard at Filibert. "You're *still* in too big of a hurry!

You have to LEARN

before you can DO?

You have to work hard

And nothing's as

Easy peasie!

as *you* seem to think!

Whatsmore, Mr. Smarty Pants, Filibert, true masterpieces are very, *very* rare.

Just look at how few paintings Johannes Vermeer painted - less than 50 in his whole life! ***And*** he was one of the greatest masters of masterpieces!

A Lady Writing - Johannes Vermeer (1665)

Johannes Vermeer, the great Dutch artist, knew that masterpieces are never - *ever* rushed or created at the snap of the fingers just because *you want* them to be.

... And, Filibert," the **Troubling Wind** frowned, shaking his head. "A little **humility** wouldn't hurt either - so - **NO** more bragging!

Filibert, you don't need to build a *grand* castle or bake the

biggest, finest pie!

Just try to do your best!"

"Looks like *I really flubbed things up!*" Filibert murmurred to himself. I should have just made cupcakes!"

Filled with the kind of **miserable embarrassment** that burns from **tip** to **toe**s, Filibert watched his guests file outside.

When he the last one disappear around the mountain bend, he roared a **stream** of --

as hot as burning -

Lava

a roar so loud and so fierce, that even the **Troubling Wind** had to hold his ears -- but to Filibert the roaring felt ***GOOD*!**

good because ...

his *fire* was as ***hot*** as melted wax

as *hot* as a frying pan

as *hot* as the **hottest red hot** candies

as *hot* as the meanest, fiercest, most terrible evil **black** dragon **breath!**

But the real truth was, Filibert knew deep down that the Troubling Wind was right - as always!

It was true.
He *had* been in too big of a hurry!

He hadn't made a plan!

He had been -

pig-headed!

Arrogant!

And, he had flown by the seat of his pants.

"If I can make fan-tab-u-lous, hats," he had wrongly reasoned ...

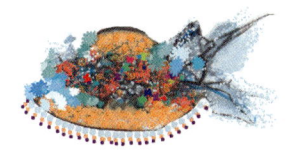

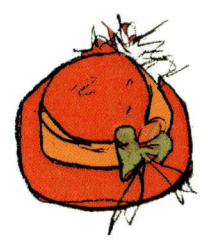

I can sure's shootin' make a silly ole pie!"

He remembered himself swaggering around bragging,

"Easy peasy!"

But -- Filibert had **not** learned how to make a proper pie!

A **scrump did dly umptious** pie!

"But ... but ...," Filibert stammered. "I didn't want to wait! I was *starving*, and I wanted **pie** right then and there!"

Besides! WHO *want*s to practice?

Practice!

Practice!

And practice some more!

BOORING!

DRUDGERY!

BLAH!

DULLSVILLE!

I wanted - no, I knew I could bake a **masterpiece**!

But the **Troubling Wind** was good and tired of listening to Filibert's excuses, so the **Troubling Wind** swirled around and blew off.

AND --

Filibert was left to *think.*

Filibert hemmed,

and **Filibert** hawed.

Filibert looked up, and Filibert looked down.

FILIBERT BAKES A PIE

Filibert looked *all* around.

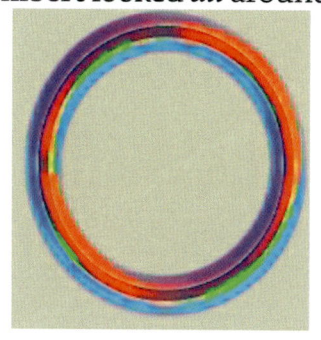

Filibert tapped his chin. And rolled his eyes!

He took a

deep - breath and, in time, Filibert began cooling off.

Finally, he decided that the *next* time he did *anything* brand new, he would *learn* how to do it - first!

35

He would start with a **plan.**

Just knowing things is great, he thought, jumping right in can be good too - but he had been too big for his britches ... he had been ...

bull-headed!

FILIBERT BAKES A PIE

Filamina was right!

He *still* had a lot of growing up to do!

Filibert's Masterpiece

Bright and early the next morning, whistling

happily, wicker basket swinging on his arm, berry thickets bursting with big, juciy **blackberries,** Filibert bound down the mountain path.

THIS time, Filibert did NOT pick the pretty green and red berries, as bright and as hard as tiny Christmas bulbs. He *only* picked the **blackest,** plumpest **berries**.

All morning, Filibert picked and picked and picked, his claws clipping and slicing and dripping with *gooey* blackberry juice. When his basket was brimming full, he skipped happily back to his lair.

Now, thanks to Mother Dragon's patient teachings, he knew how to bake a *proper* pie.

He knew -- because he had *listened.*

"*Let's start from the beginning, Filibert!*" Filibert remembered Mother Dragon's words. "**One** before **two** and **three** before **four**!"

Also Filibert remembered Mother Dragon saying that things don't always work out the first time, but that you have to have

gumption

and try, try again!

"Practice makes perfect!" Mother Dragon sang brightly, giving a *for sure* nod. "Filibert, son, we do not learn from getting things right -- but from getting things *wrong* and learning from our mistakes!"

And so, because Mother Dragon knew more about baking pies than anyone in all Dragon Land, Filibert did exactly as Mother Dragon had said.

With hats piled high on his head - for luck,

Filibert flung himself into pie making. For weeks, he practiced and practiced -- and kept practicing until there was no room left on his kitchen counter and shelves for another single pie!

FILIBERT BAKES A PIE

Filibert had made a **blueberry** pie, a **gooseberry** and a lemon with a huge merigue top, and **pumpkin**

and **rhubarb** -- and **apple** and **cherry** ...

SUZANNENSEELY

and so on! And on! And on!

Then, as a "*thank you*" for all her **loving** help, **Filibert** made **Mother Dragon** a **pecan** pie topped with big fluffy dollops of whipped cream!

"Her favorite!" he grinned ear-to-ear.

Filibert studied his pie's lovely golden browness.
His pie was *not* fancy!

His pie was humble, the kind **dragon ladies** set out on their window ledges to cool.

His pie did *not* have a crust that puffed up into a huge **golden** dome. His pie had a simple lattice crust with strips of dough that wove in and out across the top. In fact, his pie crust was even kinda *crooked*! *And* gooey **blackberry** juice had drizzled down the sides and pooled on the plate!

Filibert had to admit ...

his **blackberry pie** looked plain ole *ordinary*.

"Maybe I'll have a *pie party?*" he thought.

No!

He most certainly would *not!*

First he would take just a little taste, a teensy, weensy, tinsy "snick."

So, Filibert sliced a teensy, weensy, tinsy sliver of pie. "Just a teeny weeny tinsy snick," he muttered taking a bite.

Filibert's eyes glittered with happy tears and a **big**, proud **feeling** rose in his chest.

A **button** popped off of his **jacket** and bounced clear across the floor!

His pie was good - *really, really* **good!** **No! Doubly double good!**

Filibert's **heart** thumpety thumped for -

my **GREATEST JOY**

FILIBERT BAKES A PIE

He had created a **masterpiece!**

His *ugly* duckling pie

had turned into a *be-u-ti-ful* swan of a pie!!!

SUZANNENSEELY

Now it was time to **celebrate!**

The End
(at least *for now*)

FILIBERT'S *PIE* Recipes

SUZANNENSEELY

Filibert's **Blackberry** *Pie*

FILIBERT BAKES A PIE

1 baked pie shell
1 1/4 quart of the freshest, bestest, juciest **blackberries**
Sieve 1 cup of the **blackberries**

Combine :
1 cup water
3/4 cup sugar
2 1/2 tablespoons cornstarch
1/4 teaspoon salt
Stir together until thickened over low heat, 10 minutes:
Add sieved blackberry juice

Arrange remaining whole **berries** evenly along the bottom of pie shell. Pour syrup over berries.
 Chill pie 5 hours.
    Garnish with whipped cream - *yummiedy!*

      Yum!
      YUM!

Uncle Bucky's Rhubarb Pie

Preheat oven to 400 F

Bake pie crust to a beautiful golden **brown**, then fill with 4 cups sliced **rhubarb**

Combine, then beat together -

1 1/2 cups sugar
3 large egg **yolks**
1/2 cup all-purpose flour
3 tablespoons whole milk

3/4 teasooon nutmeg

Pour mix over **rhubarb**. Bake 400 degrees, 20 min. Reduce heat to 350, continue baking 20 minutes.

Meringue:

Add 1/4 teaspoon cream of tartar to 2 - 3 egg whites
Whip until stiff.
Tablespoon at a time, beat in 3 tablespoons sugar.
1/2 teaspoon vanilla

Spoon meringue on pie, bake until lightly browned.

Grandfather Dragon's Lemon Meringue Pie

Preheat oven to 350 F - Bake 9" pie crust to golden brown

Pie Filling
4 large egg yolks

1 cup granulated sugar
3/4 cup fresh lemon juice
2 tablespoons cornstarch
1/2 cup (1 stick sliced) chilled butter

Whisk egg yolks, eggs, sugar, lemon juice, and cornstarch in top of a double boiler. Cook medium heat, stirring constantly, until mixture coats the back of a spoon. Remove mixture from boiler. Stir in butter. Pour into baked crust.

Meringue
4 large egg whites
1/2 teaspoon cornstarch
1/4 teaspoon cream of tartar
1/2 cup superfine sugar
1 teaspoon vanilla extract
Beat egg whites until foamy. Add cornstarch and cream of tartar until soft peaks form. Gradually beat in sugar and vanilla at high speed until peaks form. Mound onto pie. Bake to a light brown

Filamina's Strawberry Cream Pie

Preheat over to 350
Bake 1 - 9 inch pie shell to a beautiful golden brown - or use a Grahm cracker crust.
Fill bottom with 1/2 cup slivered almonds and 1 1/4 cups sliced strawberries. Reserve 1 cup for glaze.

Cream filling

Mix
1/2 cup sugar
3 tablespoons cornstarch
3 tablespoons flour
1/2 teaspoons salt
Gradually stir 2 cups milk into dry ingredients, stirring constantly until mixture reaches a soft boil, reduce heat, continue cooking until thickened. Mix 1 teaspoon hot mixture into 1 beaten egg, add to milk mixture, stir until thickened. Chill. Fold in 1/2 cup whipping cream and 1 teaspoon vanilla. Spoon filling over sliced **strawberries** and slivered almonds. Top with **strawberry** slices.

Glaze

Sieve remaining **strawberries,** add 1 tbsp lemon juice, 1/2 cup water, 1/3 cup sugar, 1 tbsp cornstarch. Stir until mixture cooks clear. Add red food coloring, if necessary. Cool. Pour over pie. Refrigerate.
Garnish whipped cream

Grandmother Dragon"s Favorite - **Pecan** Pie!

1 cup light **brown** sugar, packed
1/2 cup granulated sugar
3 large eggs
1/2 tsp. salt
1/2 cup (1 stick) melted butter
1 1/2 tsp. vanilla
2 tbsp whole milk
1 tbsp flour
1 1/4 cup chopped pecans
1 unbaked 9 " deep-dish pie shell
1 cup pecan halves

FILIBERT BAKES A PIE

Preheat oven to 375
Beat both sugars with eggs until creamy, add melted butter, vanilla, milk, flour and chopped pecans. Arrange pecans evenly on botton of pie shell. Spoon mixture over top.
Bake 1 hour or until knife comes out clean
Serve warm with vanilla ice-cream or whipped cream.

Dragon Land Coconut Custard Pie

4 large eggs
3/4 cup sugar
1 1/4 tsp. vanilla
2 c whole milk
1/2 c Pancake mix
1/2 stick butter (room temperture)
3/4 cup flaked coconut

Blend all incredients
Pour in greased 10 inch pie pan
Sprinkle 1 cup coconut over top.

Bake in a preheated 350 degree F for 50-55 minutes or until knife comes out clean
Top with whipped cream

Every dragon in all Dragon Land loves this Chocolate Pie!

Heat oven to 350 degrees F.
Press 35 - 40 crushed saltine crackers into pie plate
3 tablespoons sugar
3/4 cup sugar
5 1/4 tablespoons melted butter
2 tablespoons cornstarch
Pinch of salt
1 1/2 cup milk
2 large egg yolks
4 1/2 ounces bittersweet chocolate, cut into pieces
1 teaspoon vanilla
1 tablespoon sweet butter

Pour cracker mixture into 9 inch pie plate. Mix in 3 tablespoons sugar. Pour 5 1/4 tablespoons melted butter over top. Blend saltines and butter with fork until evenly moistened. Press cracker mixture in bottom and up sides of pie pan. Bake 15 minutes.

Filling

In medium saucepan, mix 3/4 cup sugar, 2 tablespoons cornstarch and pinch of salt. Whisk together 1 1/2 cup milk and 2 large egg **yolks**, add to sugar mix. Stir over medium heat until blubbles appear around pan edges.
Cook 15 - 20 more seconds.
Remove from heat, add **chocolate** chunks, stirring until melted Stir in vanilla and **butter**. Cool. Garnish with whipped cream and chocolate curls

And then ... every everybody's *favorite ...*

Tomatoe Pie!
Oh my!

9 " pie crust, pricked and baked for 10 minutes at 400 degrees

Reduce heat to 325 degrees

5 **big ripe tomatoes** (blanch, skin, and slightly squeeze to remove excess juice)
Slice thin and layer 2 layers in pie **crust**
Sprinkle with salt and pepper
1 cup chopped **green** onions. Add 1/2 to layer of **tomatoes**
Repeat another layer of **tomatoes** and onions
1 1/2 tsp. **Oregano**, divided between tomatoe layers

Mix 2 cups of grated Sharp **Cheddar Cheese** and 1 cup mayonnaise
Put over **tomatoe** layers

Sprinkle with Parmesan Cheese Bake at 325 for 45 minutes

About the Author

Suzanne New Seely is the daughter of an Air Force fighter pilor. She was born in Ft. Worth, Texas and has lived throughout the United States and as well as Rio de Janeiro, Brazil and Madrid, Spain. Suzanne is married and has two children. She speaks Portuguese and Spanish and is an accomplished sculptor, painter, writer and interior decorator. Currently she lives in Florida.

More Books to Come!!!

Finally the End!!!!

FILIBERT BAKES A PIE

FILIBERT BAKES A PIE

SUZANNENSEELY

FILIBERT BAKES A PIE

SUZANNENSEELY

FILIBERT BAKES A PIE

SUZANNENSEELY

FILIBERT BAKES A PIE

SUZANNE SEELY

FILIBERT BAKES A PIE

!

SUZANNENSEELY

FILIBERT BAKES A PIE

SUZANNENSEELY

FILIBERT BAKES A PIE

SUZANNENSEELY

FILIBERT BAKES A PIE

Made in the USA
Columbia, SC
12 October 2024